You Know You're Having a

Senior Moment

When...

Ben Fraser

summersdale

YOU KNOW YOU'RE HAVING A SENIOR MOMENT WHEN...

Summersdale Publishers Ltd
46 West Street
Chichester
West Sussex
PO19 1RP
UK

www.summersdale.com

Printed and bound in China

ISBN: 978-1-84953-073-6

Substantial discounts on bulk quantities of Summersdale books are available to corporations, professional associations and other organisations. For details contact Summersdale Publishers by telephone: +44 (0) 1243 771107, fax: +44 (0) 1243 786300 or email: nicky@summersdale.com.

To..

From....................................

You stop on the staircase to catch your breath, and can't remember whether you were going up or down.

You ring your friend to ask them for their phone number.

You insist on handing out name badges at all family gatherings, especially Sunday lunch with your spouse and children.

You find yourself marvelling at your car's ability to move itself from where you parked it.

You realise that's Vaseline you're
spreading on your toast,
not margarine.

You find vegetable peelings in
the clothes basket, and suddenly
understand why the waste disposal
unit is blocked.

You are barred from your local supermarket for causing checkout hold-ups as you try to remember your PIN.

You answer the phone, only to discover
it wasn't your phone that was ringing
– it was on the television.

You find the presence of public toilet facilities worryingly comforting.

You are overwhelmed by the urge to
'get home, get settled into your trousers
with the elasticated waist and get the
curtains closed'.

You are annoyed by the fact that your all-in-one remote will not open your garage door. Then you see it's the phone.

In a modern art gallery, you stand for ages admiring what turns out to be... a light switch.

You acquire third-degree burns at
lunch by absentmindedly dipping your
hand in your cup of coffee for a cheese
and onion crisp.

You forget to remove your Breathe Right night-time nasal strip in the morning – and only notice when it pings off during lunch.

You suddenly wonder why there are so many cars driving on the wrong side of the road today.

You use the phrase 'the one from the TV' to describe what you're looking for in the supermarket.

You spend half an hour searching for your glasses, only to find that they were on your head the entire time.

You pop out for milk and come home
with a new dog collar, rawl plugs,
some plant pots that were on special
offer... but no milk.

You remark that you haven't
seen the Queen Mum on the TV
for a while.

You mention to Olive that you must phone Olive when you get the chance.

You insist on using your 'usual computer' at the library, since that's the one with all of your emails on.

You telephone a relative from abroad
for their full address, so you can send
a postcard and let them know how
you're getting on.

You become frustrated by instructions to 'press any key' – why would they tell you to do that when there's no 'Any' key on your keyboard?

You search high and low in the pantry cupboard and still can't find your Old Spice powder.

Your enthusiastic efforts to catch the attention of a friend in the street are met with looks of increasing terror as you draw nearer and embrace a complete stranger.

You take the bus into town and end up in the next county, with only a vague recollection of a dream involving toasted teacakes.

The strained looks on the faces of your
friends and family tell you they have
heard this story before. Many times.

You have to ask yourself, 'Do I have two cats, or three?'

Your dentist seems a bit baffled as you start to undress for your yearly check-up.

You mistake your electric blanket
kicking in for a hot flush.

You insist that Cif isn't half as good as Jif used to be.

You interrupt your third round
of hold 'em poker with a cry
of 'Blackjack!'

The local charity shop is very pleased to accept your donation of brand new clothes, still in their bags from yesterday's shopping trip.

Your 'Green Waste' recycling bin contains items such as green tea bags, salt and vinegar crisp packets and those lime-flavoured fruit gums you're not so keen on.

You look in the kitchen cupboard and wonder why that son of yours hasn't been eating his favourite breakfast cereal, and remember he left home several years ago.

You request a Ring and Ride pick-up from your address of 30 years ago.

A neighbour remarks upon how well your Marigolds complement your evening dress.

You kindly offer a guest free
choice from your bowl of
ornamental fruit.

After brushing several times with disappointing results, you read the fine print and discover that Anusol is not, in fact, a brand of toothpaste.

You require a pen and paper
to order a round of drinks.

You think Mr Bean isn't half as funny as he used to be, and then realise you're watching Gordon Brown's party address.

You can't work out how the cereal got into the fridge, and start to feel nervous about where you might find the milk.

You think you've won the lottery, only
to be informed that it's the jackpot that
rolls over, not your ticket.

Your partner's name and pets' names appear interchangeable or, worse, you resort to calling them all 'thingy'.

Every party is now a surprise party – including the ones you host.

You find yourself touching up your
car's paintwork with Fixodent.

You find yourself coating your dentures with Fix·a·dent.

You reach for your 5-iron and pull out your new, lightweight walking stick.

You're not too surprised by the financial crisis – your hairline has already been in recession for 20 years!

The petrol station attendant tells you
how much your fuel comes to, and you
think they must be selling you
another car.

You ask the gas man to wait at the door while you fetch your order for two extra semi-skimmed and a bottle of orange.

You find yourself enjoying a
healthy morning bowl of
Kitty Bites.

You decide against buying your
grandson a jigsaw puzzle labelled 2–4
years. After all, they only have two
weeks off at Christmas.

You lay the table for breakfast
straight after eating dinner.

You eventually manage to make it to the top of the ladder before it dawns on you that it's against the wrong wall.

Your friend arrives at the allotment and asks how long it has taken you to weed and hoe his patch.

You call BT to complain that your new,
high-speed wireless box can't even
get Radio 4.

You accidentally open your outgoing post and launch into a tirade about how useless Royal Mail are these days.

You catch sight of your reflection in a shop window and wonder why your coat appears to have a kink in it... only to later find that the coat hanger is still inside.

You wonder if you can travel
through the EU on your
bus pass.

No matter how much you adjust your turntable, it simply will not play your new Michael Bublé CD.

You are thoroughly disappointed to discover that Marks and Spencer's new local outlet 'Your S&M' doesn't even have a fruit and veg section.

Someone asks you how large your carbon footprint is, and you reply, 'I wiped my feet as I came in, thank you very much!'

You spend the afternoon going through old photo albums, but can't remember who any of the people are in the pictures.

After queuing for half an hour to buy
stamps in the Post Office, you forget to
stick them on any of your letters.

You resort to opening a child-proof lid with a mallet.

The crocheted bobble hat you're
wearing looks remarkably like your
tea cosy.

Today's newspaper seems strangely
familiar – they've even repeated
yesterday's front page headline!

You stop to admire the snowy hills in view of your house and discover (after five years of living there) that they are chalk cliffs.

Your dilemma concerning whether
you should have taken the white
or the blue pill tonight comes to an
embarrassingly pointed conclusion at
your friends' dinner party.

You get accusing looks from parents in the playground as you cheerily sing Gary Glitter's 'Do You Wanna Be in My Gang?', but you don't quite know why.

You decide it's time to pull up your socks, and realise you forgot to put any on.

Have you enjoyed this book?
If so, why not write a review
on your favourite website?

Thanks very much for buying
this Summersdale book.

www.summersdale.com